W9-CPE-961

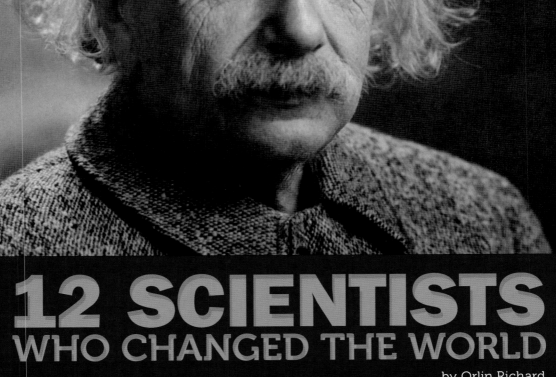

12 SCIENTISTS
WHO CHANGED THE WORLD

by Orlin Richard

12 STORY LIBRARY

www.12StoryLibrary.com

12-Story Library is an imprint of Peterson Publishing Company and Press Room Editions.

Produced for 12-Story Library by Red Line Editorial

Photographs ©: Orren Jack Turner/Library of Congress, cover, 1, 14; Claudio Zaccherini/ Shutterstock Images, 4; Morphart Creation/Shutterstock Images, 5; Bill Meeks/AP Images, 6, 28; 2xSamara.com/Shutterstock Images, 7; Frances Benjamin Johnston/Library of Congress, 8; Amawasri Pakdara/Shutterstock Images, 9; Bettmann/Corbis, 10; Underwood & Underwood/Corbis, 11; Library of Congress, 12, 18; BlueOrange Studio/Shutterstock Images, 13; Corbis, 16; Everett Historical/Shutterstock Images, 17; Bettmann/Corbis/AP Images, 19; Rick Rycroft/AP Images, 20, 29; apple2499/Shutterstock Images, 21; James McArdell/Library of Congress, 22; Bain News Service/Library of Congress, 24, 26; Baloncici/ Shutterstock Images, 25; Vladislav Proshkin/Shutterstock Images, 27

ISBN
978-1-63235-149-4 (hardcover)
978-1-63235-190-6 (paperback)
978-1-62143-242-5 (hosted ebook)

Library of Congress Control Number: 2015934295

Printed in the United States of America
Mankato, MN
June, 2015

Go beyond the book. Get free, up-to-date content on this topic at 12StoryLibrary.com.

TABLE OF CONTENTS

ARCHIMEDES EXPERIMENTS WITH FLOTATION

Archimedes created mathematical rules and inventions that we still use today. He was born in Syracuse, Sicily, in what is now Italy. He was born sometime between 290 and 280 BCE. Archimedes studied in Egypt but lived most of his life in Syracuse. He died in approximately 212 BCE.

Like other ancient scientists, Archimedes studied many different things. He believed strongly in experimentation. He created many different machines. One machine is called Archimedes' screw. It moves water from one place to another. It is a tube set at a 45-degree angle. Inside the tube is a screw. As the screw turns, water moves up the tube. It is pushed out the other end. It was used to remove water from inside large ships.

Archimedes was a mathematician in ancient Italy.

THINK ABOUT IT

Archimedes and other ancient scientists studied many different things. Why do you think scientists in the ancient world studied many different subjects instead of just one?

9
Number of Archimedes' formal papers that have survived.

- Archimedes was born in Syracuse, Sicily, between 290 and 280 BCE.
- He discovered many geometric and mathematical principles.
- He invented machines such as Archimedes' screw that are still used today.

Versions of the screw are still used today.

Archimedes is most famous for Archimedes' principle. It explains what makes things float. It also explains why some things float while others do not.

Archimedes made many other discoveries in mathematics, geometry, and physics. European mathematicians rediscovered his work in the 1500s. It helped develop the future of mathematics. His discoveries have become the basis for much of modern science.

EUREKA!

A popular story about Archimedes claims he discovered Archimedes' principle in the bathtub. He supposedly jumped out of the bath and shouted, "Eureka!" *Eureka* means "I have found it" in ancient Greek. "Eureka" is now something people say when they make a discovery.

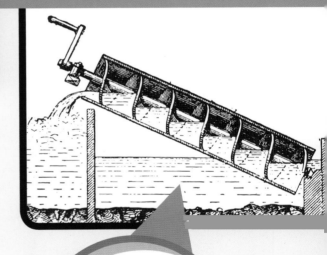

Archimedes' screw moves water from one location to another.

5

NORMAN BORLAUG SAVES BILLIONS OF LIVES

Norman Borlaug was a leading scientist in the study of plants. He was born in the farming town of Cresco, Iowa, in 1914. He worked on his parents' farm. He learned to work hard. Borlaug was the first person in his family to go to college. He studied agricultural science at the University of Minnesota.

After graduating, Borlaug worked in Mexico. Farmers there could not grow enough food. The wheat they grew was not strong enough. It could not survive disease and the weather. The farmers were not growing enough food to feed all of Mexico's people.

Borlaug came up with a way to fix the problem. He created a new type of wheat by breeding different types together. The new wheat resisted disease. It did not bend over in the wind. With the new wheat, Mexican

Borlaug created different types of wheat.

farmers could produce enough food. They were able to feed Mexico's people by 1956.

Borlaug's new wheat spread across the world. Billions of people were fed who otherwise might have starved. Borlaug received the Nobel Peace Prize in 1970 for the lives he saved.

Because of Borlaug's work, wheat grows in difficult areas, such as mountains.

198 million

Approximate number of acres (80 million ha) planted with wheat varieties Borlaug's work helped develop.

- Borlaug was born in Cresco, Iowa, in 1914.
- He created a new type of wheat that resisted disease and grew in different climates.
- In 1970, Borlaug received the Nobel Peace Prize for the lives he saved.

3

GEORGE WASHINGTON CARVER IMPROVES FARMING

George Washington Carver did not have the education of most scientists. Carver was born in Missouri in approximately 1865. His parents were slaves. When Carver was young, he and his mother were kidnapped. He was returned to the farm where he was born. But his mother was not. Farm owners Moses and Susan Carver raised young George.

Carver developed ways to help farmers grow more crops.

300

Number of new products Carver made from peanuts.

- Carver was born in Missouri in approximately 1865.
- He studied agriculture and used his knowledge to develop new plant products and farming methods.
- He died in 1943. His monument was the first to honor an African American.

Carver transformed peanuts into many different products.

Carver was often ill as a child. He spent time with Susan doing household chores. He helped her tend the garden. Susan taught him to read and write. When he grew older, he traveled around the Midwest. He worked and went to different schools. Eventually, Carver attended the State Agricultural College in Iowa. He studied plants and agriculture. Carver took a job teaching and researching at Tuskegee Institute in Alabama.

He used his knowledge of plants to make new things. He came up with new uses for peanuts, sweet potatoes, soybeans, and many other plants. He made cheese, soap, and grease from peanuts. Carver helped poor Southern farmers use science to produce larger and better crops. The poor farmers made more money. Carver died in 1943. After his death, President Franklin Roosevelt dedicated a monument to him. It was the first US monument to honor an African American.

9

MARIE CURIE HARNESSES RADIOACTIVITY

Maria Salomea Skłodowska was born in Warsaw, Poland, in 1867. She moved to Paris, France, in 1891 to study at the Sorbonne University. While there, she changed her name to Marie. She studied physics and math. She was one of the best students at the school in both fields.

She met Pierre Curie in 1894. They married the next year. Pierre was also a scientist. They worked together. The Curies were interested

Curie at work in her laboratory

in radioactivity. It was discovered by Henri Becquerel in 1896.

Pierre and Marie Curie discovered radium and polonium.

Together, the Curies discovered the element polonium. Marie named it after her homeland of Poland. The Curies also discovered the element radium. Radium and polonium were both radioactive. The Curies shared a Nobel Prize for their work with Becquerel in 1903. Marie was the first woman to win a Nobel Prize.

Pierre died in 1906. Marie took over his professorship. She became the first woman to teach at the

Sorbonne. In 1911, she received her second Nobel Prize. It awarded her study of radium.

During World War I (1914–1918), Curie developed X-radiography. It was used to see inside a patient's body. X-rays are still used in medicine today. The discovery has saved many lives.

2
Number of times Curie won the Nobel Prize.

- Curie was born Maria Salomea Skłodowska in Warsaw, Poland, in 1867.
- She discovered the elements radium and polonium and studied radioactivity and its medical uses.
- She died from cancer caused by radioactivity in 1934.

Curie continued to research, lecture, and experiment for the rest of her life. She died in 1934 from leukemia. The cancer was caused by her long exposure to radioactivity. At the time, people did not know radioactivity was harmful. But she had forever transformed the scientific fields she studied.

CHARLES DARWIN DISCOVERS THE ORIGIN OF SPECIES

Few scientists have had the far-reaching impact Charles Darwin has. Darwin's father sent him to study medicine at Edinburgh University in 1825. At Edinburgh, Darwin learned much about animals and the natural world. He became curious about where different species came from.

> Darwin's theories would change the world's understanding of how species change over time.

In 1831, Darwin took a trip that would change the world. He set sail on a ship called the *Beagle*. It traveled from England to South America, Australia, and Africa. Darwin studied the plants and animals wherever the *Beagle* stopped. He started to shape his ideas on evolution.

Darwin returned to England and wrote about his theory of natural selection. The theory said that creatures with more advantageous traits lived longer. They passed these traits to the next generation. Darwin wrote about his theory. His book *On the Origin of Species by Means of Natural Selection* was published in 1859.

5

Number of years Darwin's *Beagle* voyage lasted.

- Darwin was born in England in 1809 and studied at Edinburgh University.
- He came up with the theory of natural selection.
- He published his theory in his book *On the Origin of Species by Means of Natural Selection*.

THINK ABOUT IT

Darwin's theories challenged what religions taught about where life came from. How do you think religious leaders reacted to Darwin's theories? Do you think they embraced the theories or spoke out against them?

Darwin's ideas on natural selection and evolution changed the world. It changed how scientists thought about where life came from. He revolutionized nearly every field of social and physical science. He changed how people understand the world.

Blue-footed boobies are just one species Darwin studied on his trip on the *Beagle*.

ALBERT EINSTEIN STUDIES SPACE AND TIME

Albert Einstein came from humble beginnings. He was born in Ulm, Germany, in 1879. As a young boy, Einstein was interested in how compasses work. He studied the invisible forces that made compass needles move. He came across a geometry book and read it cover to cover.

In 1905, Einstein had what is called his miracle year. He was only 26.

Einstein was one of the world's most influential scientists.

1921

Year Einstein was awarded the Nobel Prize in theoretical physics.

- Einstein was born in Germany in 1879.
- He came up with important theories on relativity and the photoelectric effect.
- He fled Nazi Germany in the 1930s and lived the rest of his life in the United States.

He published four physics papers that changed the field forever. These papers described general and special relativity. Einstein's general relativity theory says the laws of gravity break down when gravity becomes very strong. His special relativity theory says the laws of motion break down as they reach the speed of light. Einstein's papers also described something called the photoelectric effect. It occurs when a material absorbs a type of radiation.

Einstein, a Jew, fled Germany in 1932. The Nazis were rising to power in Germany. They hated the Jews. They wanted to remove them from Germany. He went to the United States, where he lived until his death in 1955. Einstein never returned to Germany. He taught physics at Princeton University. He helped convince President Franklin Roosevelt to fund a special project. It led to the creation of the atomic bomb. Einstein would later regret contributing to the creation of the powerful weapon.

Scientists today are still trying to prove Einstein's theories. Many think Einstein was ahead of his time. He predicted gravitational waves, black holes, and other things scientists are now discovering in space. Einstein was one of the most influential scientists of all time.

7

ALEXANDER FLEMING ACCIDENTLY DISCOVERS PENICILLIN

Not all great scientific discoveries come from years of study. Some are just happy accidents. Alexander Fleming was a great scientist. But his greatest discovery happened by accident. Fleming discovered the antibiotic penicillin. The medicine has saved millions of lives. It was perhaps the greatest medical discovery of the twentieth century.

Fleming was born in Scotland in 1881. He studied to become a doctor. Fleming served in the medical corps during World War I (1914–1918). Afterwards, he became a professor of bacteriology. Bacteriology is the study of the tiny organisms that live in the human body. Bacteria is the cause of many diseases.

Fleming in his laboratory in London, England

Penicillin mold growing in a flask

One day in 1928, Fleming was studying bacteria in his lab. He noticed one sample of bacteria had been infected by a mold called *Penicillium notatum.* The mold had stopped the bacteria from growing. Fleming theorized that the mold might have a medical use. It could be used to treat disease. The medicine came to be called *penicillin* after the mold that it came from. It was one of the first antibiotics. Fleming shared a Nobel Prize with two other scientists in 1945 for the discovery and development of penicillin.

15

Years between Fleming's discovery of penicillin and the drug's mass production in 1943.

- Fleming was born in Scotland in 1881.
- He studied medicine and served as a doctor in World War I.
- He became a professor of bacteriology and discovered penicillin.

GALILEO GALILEI LOOKS TO THE STARS

Galileo Galilei was born in 1564 in Italy. Galileo studied math and philosophy at the University of Pisa. Later, Galileo moved around Italy studying and teaching math. He wrote papers on gravity, math, motion, and astronomy.

Galileo made his own telescope and believed the earth circled around the sun.

COPERNICUS

Galileo was not the first scientist to claim the earth revolved around the sun. Polish astronomer Nicolaus Copernicus was the first to make that claim. The idea came to be known as Copernican theory. But Copernicus did not face the challenge from the Church that Galileo later did. He died just two months after he published his theory.

20

Number of degrees Galileo's telescopes magnified distant things.

- Galileo built and improved his own telescope, leading to many discoveries about space and the solar system.
- He also contributed to the fields of motion, materials, and mathematics.
- He had to take back his theory that the earth circled around the sun.

Galileo's telescope

Galileo used a telescope to make his important astronomical discoveries. He heard about a device used in the Netherlands to see faraway things. Soon, Galileo figured out how to make his own telescope. He used it to study space. He used stronger lenses to make the telescope more powerful. Galileo discovered four of Jupiter's moons.

In the sixteenth century, most people believed the sun revolved around the earth. Galileo challenged this belief. He said the earth revolved around the sun. But this went against the Catholic Church's view that the sun circles around the earth. The Church said Galileo's views were heretical. It forced Galileo to formally take back his claims. He worked for the rest of his life studying motion and the strength of materials. Galileo died in 1642.

JANE GOODALL LIVES AMONG THE CHIMPANZEES

British animal behaviorist Jane Goodall never went to college. Instead, she worked odd jobs until she became an assistant to Louis Leakey. Leakey was an anthropologist and paleontologist studying in Africa.

> Goodall's work has helped scientists understand chimpanzees better.

Goodall was 26 when she arrived in what is now Tanzania in 1960. What she lacked in formal education she made up for in passion. That same year, Goodall established the Gombe Stream Game Reserve. It would become one of Tanzania's national parks.

The park allowed her to watch chimpanzee behavior up close. She even lived among the chimpanzees. Doing so helped her understand their behavior. Goodall discovered chimpanzees eat both meat and vegetables. She found that they use tools. Scientists used to think that only humans did that. Her greatest discovery was the chimpanzees'

complicated social behaviors. They were more than simple animals.

For more than 50 years, Goodall has continued to study the chimpanzees at the park. Goodall changed how humans think about their relationships with other creatures. She showed how alike humans and chimpanzees are. Her work continues to show why the natural world is worth studying.

1968

Year the Gombe Stream National Park was established.

- Goodall traveled to Africa as an assistant to Louis Leakey.
- She established a camp to study chimpanzees.
- She learned much about how chimpanzees lived and proved they were complicated creatures.

Goodall observed chimpanzees acting in ways similar to humans.

ISAAC NEWTON DESCRIBES THE LAWS OF THE UNIVERSE

Physicist and mathematician Isaac Newton was born in England in 1643. He was inspired by the work of Galileo. He used Galileo's theories to come up with his own laws of motion.

A popular myth claims Newton came up with his theories of gravity and acceleration when an apple fell on his head. This story is likely false. But watching

Newton discovered the laws of motion and gravity.

3

Number of laws of motion Newton discovered.

- Newton was inspired by the work of Galileo.
- He is credited with discovering gravity.
- He wrote about gravity and his three laws of motion in his famous book, *The Mathematical Principles of Natural Philosophy.*

THE ROYAL SOCIETY OF LONDON

The Royal Society of London is a club for scientists. Members gather and discuss new theories and ideas. They promote new research. The society began in 1660. Some of the greatest scientists of all time were members. Isaac Newton, Charles Darwin, and many others were Royal Society members.

apples fall from trees may have inspired these discoveries. Newton furthered the scientific understanding of light and gravity. He came up with explanations for how the planets moved in space. His most important work was *The Mathematical Principles of Natural Philosophy*. It is one of the most important books in modern science. It discussed his laws of motion and gravity. Newton's laws of motion describe how and why objects move. His law of gravity describes how objects on Earth and in space are attracted to one another. His book made Newton one

of the most famous scientists in the world.

Newton was one of two scientists to independently invent calculus in the 1600s. Calculus is an advanced field of mathematics. It has made many things possible, from space travel to computers. Without Newton's contributions, much of modern science would not exist.

LOUIS PASTEUR EXPLORES GERM THEORY

Few scientists have a process named after them. But chemist Louis Pasteur is one of them. The process of pasteurization is named after Pasteur. He discovered it in the nineteenth century. His medical discoveries and innovations saved countless lives.

In 1854, Pasteur became a chemistry professor at the University of Lille in France. He researched fermentation. Fermentation is the process by which alcohol is made. He discovered that microorganisms caused fermentation. This was called the germ theory of fermentation.

Pasteur used his knowledge of fermentation to prevent wine and other liquids from spoiling. Pasteur heated up the liquid enough to kill the organisms that caused it to spoil. Today this process is called pasteurization. It makes all kinds of drinks, including milk, safer to drink.

Pasteur researched the process of fermentation.

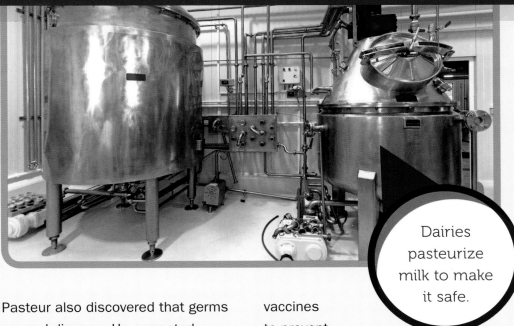

Dairies pasteurize milk to make it safe.

Pasteur also discovered that germs caused disease. He promoted the idea that fighting germs could prevent illness. He helped develop vaccines to prevent diseases. Vaccines help fight diseases from rabies to polio. Pasteur's research still impacts how doctors study disease today.

145

Temperature, in degrees Fahrenheit (63° C), at which milk is pasteurized in the United States today.

- Pasteur discovered germ theory.
- He developed pasteurization, a way to prevent fermentation by heating liquids that could spoil.
- He was one of the first scientists to study and develop vaccines.

MIASMA THEORY

Before germ theory, there were many different ideas about what caused disease. Many thought diseases were caused by contact with "bad air." People thought getting rid of the bad smells in the air would get rid of disease. This was known as miasma theory.

NIKOLA TESLA ELECTRIFIES THE WORLD

Nikola Tesla studied electricity. He was born in 1856 in what is now Croatia. He studied engineering in Austria and Prague. In Graz, Austria, Tesla saw an electric generator and motor. It inspired him to develop alternating current. Alternating current is electricity that can be used in many different sizes of homes and businesses.

In 1884, Tesla moved to the United States. He worked with famous inventor Thomas Edison. But the two men did not get along. Tesla struck out on his own. He invented the Tesla coil in 1891. The coil is now used to make radios, televisions, and other electronics work. Tesla also invented a remote-controlled boat, human-made lightning, and many other devices.

Tesla invented alternating current.

Tesla helped make electricity useable for everyone. But he made strange claims toward the end of his life. He believed he had received radio contact from another world. He claimed to have made a death ray that could destroy 10,000 airplanes from 250 miles (400 km) away. Despite his strange beliefs at the end of his life, Tesla was a great nineteenth-century scientist. His inventions made much of the modern world possible.

Tesla coils are still used today.

$1.37 million

Amount raised in an Internet campaign to fund a Tesla museum in 2012.

- Tesla was born in 1856 in modern Croatia.
- He invented alternating current, the Tesla coil, and more.
- He held shows to demonstrate the safety of the alternating current.

ALTERNATING CURRENT

People thought Tesla's alternating current might be dangerous. To prove it was safe, Tesla held public demonstrations. He allowed alternating current to be run through his body. He was unharmed. This showed people that alternating current was safe for use at home.

27

HOW YOU CAN MAKE CHANGE

Attend a Science Fair

Scientists make change by coming up with new ideas and testing them. Try out your experiments by entering them in a local science fair. With the help of an adult, search online to find a local science fair and put your best project forward. Get inspired by other scientists your age by checking out other science fair exhibits.

Visit a University

With an adult, visit a local university. Often, university students hold events to show off their research. Speak with the students to learn about what it is like to study science. Come up with your own idea for a research project.

Volunteer in Your Town

There are lots of opportunities for studying science in your hometown. Volunteer with an adult at an animal shelter to learn how animals behave. Help clean up a local river or park and discover why it is important to keep the environment around you clean.

GLOSSARY

advantageous
Increasing the chances of success.

agricultural science
The study of crops and farming.

astronomy
The study of the stars and space.

atomic bomb
A bomb that produces an incredibly strong explosion.

breeding
Mixing different plants together to create a new type.

element
A substance that cannot be separated into smaller, simpler substances.

evolution
The transformation of a species of plant or animal over time.

experimentation
Trying something many times in different ways to find out how it works or make it work better.

heretical
Against the teachings of a church.

microorganisms
Tiny living things that can only be seen through a microscope.

radioactivity
Giving off energy by breaking apart certain elements.

species
Different types of animals and plants.

vaccines
Substances injected into people or animals to protect them against disease.

FOR MORE INFORMATION

Books

Farndon, John. *Great Scientists*. New York: Sandy Creek, 2013.

Krull, Kathleen. *Lives of the Scientists: Experiments, Explosions (and What the Neighbors Thought)*. New York: Harcourt Children's Books, 2013.

Steele, Philip. *Isaac Newton: The Scientist Who Changed Everything*. Washington, DC: National Geographic Society, 2007.

Websites

Kids.gov: Inventors and Scientists
www.kids.usa.gov/science/scientists/index.shtml

Science Kids: Famous Scientist Facts
www.sciencekids.co.nz/sciencefacts/scientists.html

Scientists and Inventors Biographies for Kids
www.ducksters.com/biography/scientists/scientists_and_inventors.php

INDEX

About the Author

Orlin Richard grew up in Fargo, North Dakota. He has been told he bears a striking resemblance to physicist Niels Bohr.

READ MORE FROM 12-STORY LIBRARY

Every 12-Story Library book is available in many formats, including Amazon Kindle and Apple iBooks. For more information, visit your device's store or 12StoryLibrary.com.